REKINDLING THE FAITH

HOW THE IRISH RECHRISTIANISED EUROPE

SEAN McMAHON

MERCIER PRESS

For Art Byrne

Mercier Press
PO Box 5 5 French Church Street Cork
16 Hume Street Dublin 2

First published 1996

A CIP record for this book is available from the British Library.

ISBN 1 85635 143 2
10 9 8 7 6 5 4 3 2 1

Cover illustration by Eorna Walton; cover design by Bluett
Typeset by Richard Parfrey
Printed in Ireland by ColourBooks Baldoyle Dublin 13

CONTENTS

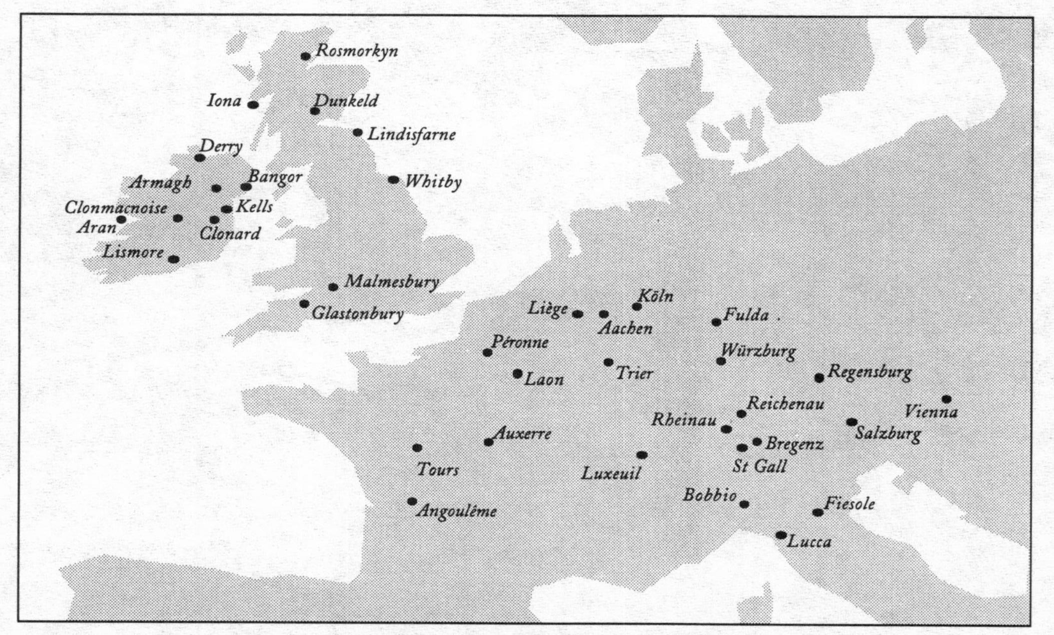

Irish monastic influence in Europe

INTRODUCTION

By the beginning of the fifth century AD the great empire of Rome was tottering; in the phrase which has come down from those times, the barbarian was at the gate. At its zenith at the death of the emperor Trajan (*c.* 53–117) the *imperium Romanum* had stretched from the Firth of Forth to the Upper Nile, from Morocco to the Persian Gulf. It incorporated all of western Europe (except *Hibernia*) and the Middle East as far as the Caspian Sea. It included the territory of twenty-five modern countries and had a population of fifty million people. All who weren't slaves could move about freely without passports from Chester to Athens, from Lusitania (modern Portugal) to the Nile, and use either of the two universal languages, Latin or Greek. Throughout these vast dominions the ideal of '*pax Romana*' usually prevailed side by side with splendid roads, bridges and aqueducts, excellent plumbing, urban amenities and what could have been but was not a first-rate legal system and civil service. These remarkable amenities were maintained in spite of – or perhaps because of – the inertia of the central government, which left the management of the distant provinces to local administrators called procurators who literally had not got enough staff. The civilisation was in reality upheld by responsible individuals who maintained the cities of the empire out of their own pockets and a sense of civic virtue.

Many explanations have been advanced for this empire's

decline and fall: the loss of *gravitas* and other stoical virtues, climatic change, lead poisoning from the pipes necessary to the excellent plumbing, overdependence on slaves, decadence at home and the use of mercenaries abroad. The most likely reason was what Ovid, one of its livelier poets, called *tempus edax rerum* ('time the devourer of everything'). It was no longer possible to police so great a dominion without help from the very barbarians who would soon end the civilisation.

The word 'barbarian' was not coined in terror; it originated from the Greek word 'barbaros' which meant literally 'stammering' and was a comment upon the incomprehensibility of the language of the lesser breeds without the law. They came mainly from the plains of north Europe and Asia and were called different names: Huns, Ostrogoths, Visigoths, Franks, Angles, Saxons, Jutes, Vandals. Their way of life was different from that of Greece or Rome, their rulers were superior warriors in a warrior state and their power was dependent on what booty they could distribute. From as early as 200 AD, they had been making plunder raids on the overextended empire but by the beginning of the fifth century they wanted land and they took it.

In anticipation of the occlusion of the territories of the west, the emperor Constantine, who claimed to be a Christian, moved his capital to Byzantium. This he modestly renamed Constantinopole and in 364 he divided the dominions into a western empire, with its capital at Rome, and the Byzantine empire (called after the old name of its capital) which he kept for himself and his descendants. This empire of the east actually survived until it fell to the Turks under Mehmed II (1429–81) in 1453. The power of Rome, as opposed to the eastern empire, waned rapidly after the split, which was made final in 395: the Goths overran Greece and Italy, sacking the eternal city in 410, and finally settled in Spain; the Vandals conquered Italy and the Huns raided Gaul. The last emperor of Rome, Romulus Augustulus, was deposed by Odoacer, king of the Goths, in 476.

Christianity had been tolerated since 313 and in all parts of the Roman dominions there were churches, hierarchical structures to run them and even heresies. At first regarded as cranks whose god had died the death of a common criminal, and socially as solemn and antisocial prudes who took no part in the games and entertainments that were put on to placate the unruly mob, the Christians were eventually tolerated. They suffered occasional savage persecutions but these were mainly spontaneous attacks on an easily identifiable minority in cities. Persecution was rarely government policy until 303 when under Diocletian there were many deaths. This policy reflected the perceived increase in population numbers and general urban unrest. Official persecution ceased when the emperor was forced to abdicate two years later, and ultimately served only to increase Christian strength and prestige. Diocletian's second successor, Constantine, whose mother Helena was a Christian, uttered an edict of toleration in 313. The persecutions were confined mainly to Rome and had little effect on the more distant provinces.

Patrick, the premier apostle to the Irish, born sometime in the last decade of the fourth century, was the son of a British deacon. It was in his boyhood (410) that the Roman legions marched away, required elsewhere by the emperor Honorius, who left the Britons with little more than the terse advice: 'Defend yourselves.' By 430 a leader, Vortigern, had appeared, with a mission to defend Britain from the barbarian raiders who literally came from all directions. Ireland was not at risk; the Irish Sea was to be an effective barrier until a later wave of barbarian invasions in the ninth and tenth centuries brought the Vikings. In fact the Irish were the western attackers of Britain, adding their raids to those of the Picts from the north and the Germans from the east. Vortigern tried the Roman trick of offering rewards of riches and land to Germans to defend the Britons against other Germans. The result was predictable; as Rudyard Kipling was to say about later invaders:

> . . . if once you have paid him the Dane-geld
> You never get rid of the Dane.

Britain became a German colony with Angles in the north and northeast, Saxons in the south and Jutes in Kent; and the practice of Christianity retreated to the western fringes.

Like Britain, most of modern France, Germany and northern Italy effectively reverted to paganism. *Pax Romana,* which had a significant admixture of *pax Christi,* was a lost dream. It was only the Church (where it was allowed to exist) that was able to preserve the grandeur and glory of classical antiquity. The New Learning of the Renaissance tended to refer to the period as the Dark Ages. Renaissance scholars considered it an era of intellectual nullity and endemic savagery. It is true that the fifth and sixth centuries, with their tribal wars, fratricidal struggles and violence, were not periods that encouraged art and science. With the twilight of the western empire knowledge and skills were lost, or at least mislaid. Yet the barbarian hordes, once they ceased their migrations (and stopped deforming the shapes of their heads to make them more fearsome as warriors), settled down to form states of greater or lesser size. Peace (or a tolerable level of violence) and a chauvinism stimulated by trade with other countries restored respect for learning. Though lacking the Mediterranean climate and temper, northern kingdoms in time established workable civilisations which led in the course of time to 'modern' attitudes. In western Europe, the Middle Ages (the period in the 'middle' between the age of classical learning and the 'restored' humanism of the Renaissance) were not really a dark interval between the death of knowledge and its rebirth but a period of conservation and continuity. In spite of lives that seemed 'solitary, poor, nasty, brutish and short', the era was characterised by a steady growth of recovered learning, informed by Christian virtues and secure in the careful and largely honourable hands of the Church. In this work of preservation and transmission the Irish saints and scholars played a major part.

By the end of the troubled fifth century, Ireland was Christian and already strongly inclined to the monasticism that was to be its glory and an occasion of later conflict with the episcopal universal Church. The source of this way of life which seemed to appeal deeply to the Celtic psyche was remotely the practice of the Desert Fathers of Egypt and proximately the rule established by such *sancti* as Ninian of Whithorn and Illtud of Caldey. It was characterised by austerity and a clear desire for solitude; even in community the monks left their individual beehive huts only for work, food and choir. Some were driven to extremes in the search for isolation, finding it in deep woods or river bends or offshore islands like Aran and Tory – or on Sceilg Mhichíl, a bare sea rock. The Latin language that came with the faith gave a means to put on vellum the hero tales of the Celts, and in the half-uncial script a beautiful hand in which to write them. The monks copied the scriptures in illuminated manuscripts which are still breathtaking, taught the sons of the rich, both Irish and European, and helped to preserve the ancient classics. Teaching, studying the scriptures, copying, labouring in field and forge, fasting and praising God made the year pass quickly but these men in their rough clothes and unflattering frontal tonsures (*ab aure usque ad aurem* – 'from ear to ear') had still time to note the season's changes and write exquisite vernacular poetry about it.

The societal patterns of Irish life laid great stress on kinship and local allegiance – a system baffling in its complexity, but one which meant that exile even within the bounds of Ireland was a particularly painful idea. This was what was called *bán-martra* – 'white martyrdom' – when a person 'renounces everything he loves for God'. The extreme austerity of monastic life, including deliberately unappetising food in small amounts and physical punishment of slaps and punches, was nothing compared to the prospect of leaving home and family. The turning of the screw that led to this final sacrifice meant exquisite pain, especially to those who left Ireland for good – the *peregrini* – and faced the terrors of primitive travel among even more primitive peoples. Their going was approved by governing abbots but not induced by them. There was no central agency, no missionary headquarters and no official connection between home and foreign foundations. The break was complete and there was no prospect of return. These *peregrinatores pro Christo* ('exiles for Christ') departed in response to an apparently personal divine call, moved to a location that seemed appropriate for the setting up of a monastery, and preached the gospel to the pagan inhabitants.

The effect was to light up what the Irish monks saw as infidel darkness and bring the gentleness of Christian practice among people whose respect for life and limb was slight. The overriding motive was almost certainly a self-inflicted mortification of the severest kind, though some may have accepted the doom imposed by a confessor as penance. The traditional, if unlikely, story of Colum Cille's leaving for Iona was that his confessor Molaise sent him to Pictland to win as many souls for Christ as were killed at the battle of Cuildremhne in 561. As a sorely offended and irascible aristocrat Colum Cille was able to lead an army against the high king, who had confiscated the copy of Finnian's psalter that the saint had made. According to the story 3,000 souls were slain and the 'first exile' left Devenish, the site of Molaise's cell on Lough Erne, to go to Derry on the first stage of his penitential journey. What is certain is that two years after the battle he and twelve apostolic companions sailed for Scotland, thus setting a pattern in numbers and purpose for later *peregrini*.

The places chosen for this spontaneous missionary work were (apart from modern Scotland) Wales, England, France, Belgium, Germany, Switzerland, Austria and Italy. Some monks penetrated beyond the Faroes to Iceland and others found their way as far east as Jerusalem and Kiev in central Russia but their main concentration was in the territory roughly between the Seine and the Rhine and along the Danube. The great names were Colum Cille, Aidan, Finan, Columban, Fursa, Goban, Gall, Kilian, Fergil and Fridian and the litany of their foundations is a roll-call of places of sanctity and learning: Iona, Lindisfarne, Whitby, Glastonbury, Peronne, Liège, Cologne, Luxeuil, Vienna, Salzburg, Würzburg, Regensburg, St Gall, Bobbio, Fiesole and at least a score more. The route to Europe lay through Britain by channel ports and penetration into the pagan land of the Franks was by coracle against the stream of north-flowing rivers. Consciously following Christ's example, these bands of determined men took little apart from precious religious books and objects. Land journeys were on foot unless they fell in with trade caravans. They journeyed until they found a location they felt suitable, hoped for a grant of a little land from a not unfriendly chief and set up their holy ground to the glory of God and (though it would not have occurred to them) the honour of Ireland.

The work they started was continued by others, notably

missionaries from Britain and the Mediterranean countries. The labours of the Irish monks in northern Britain were complemented by the Italian Augustine of Canterbury (d. 605) who arrived in Kent in 597 and soon re-Christianised the south. His brand of faith, though essentially the same as that of the Celtic churches, differed in some details, notably in its strong 'Roman' influence and its preference for an episcopal and diocesan structure. Relations were not always diplomatic and the strength of personality of the Irishmen and the Celtic character of their foundations eventually led to the famous Paschal controversy between the *Romani* and the *Hibernenses* that was settled only with extreme difficulty and not without stormy dissent in 664 at Whitby.

As time passed the nature of the *peregrini* changed. Originally they were more *sancti* than *docti* and concerned with sacred rather than profane knowledge. Columban and his brothers were no less learned than holy but their priority, after self-sanctification, was preaching the gospel. By the middle of the eighth century there was a noticeable change in motivation, approach and intellectual wares. The Carolingian dynasty was founded in 751 by Pepin III, the son of Charles Martel, who had stopped the march of Islam at Poitiers in 732. Under Pepin's son, Charlemagne (747–814), the rule became firmly Christian and the court at Aachen gained a reputation for learning, supplied largely by Irish scholars. (Charlemagne's 'minister of culture' Alcuin (*c.* 737–804), though born in Northumbria, was of Irish education.) The names of Sedulius Scottus, John Scottus Eriugena and

Dicuil are nearly as famous as those of Columban and Gall, but it was in philosophy rather than kerygma that they made their reputations, and if anyone in Charlemagne's kingdom knew Greek he was assumed to be Irish.

By the twelfth century the rule of Benedict, modified by other orders to their own needs, was universally accepted as the appropriate one for monastic houses. The Celtic pattern was gradually erased; even the *Schottenklöster* ('"Irish" monasteries'), as a number of houses in Germany and Austria which developed from a mother house in Regensburg after 1089 were called, followed the Benedictine rule. They continued to draw their postulants largely from Ireland until laxity and irregularity brought them under papal censure; by the middle of the sixteenth century they were Irish only in name. At home the great days of the Celtic monasteries were over. The Viking raids had dealt them mortal blows and such reformers as Malachy (1094–1148) and Laurence O'Toole (1130–80) had at last established a firm Roman, episcopal and diocesan rule in the anomalous western isle. The Irish monasteries would from then on be European, at first Cistercian and supplemented later by Dominican and Franciscan houses.

For six centuries, however, Ireland, through her *peregrini,* exerted a religious and cultural influence over a large part of Europe. It was due to their efforts that the west recovered from largely nihilistic and materialist pagan attitudes and began to benefit from recovered learning. Their profane work, which consisted of the custody and safe transmission of antique learning, would not have been possible without their sacred commitment. It is no exaggeration to claim that men like Colum Cille and Columban, and later Eriugena, were as necessary to what we incorrectly call the 'new' learning as Dante or Erasmus, and their Christian teaching at least blunted the savagery of many rulers and their enthusiastic minions who would undoubtedly have prolonged the darkness.

The gazetteer which follows gives biographies of the main players, both clerical and lay, in this drama of recovery, and accounts of the establishments that flamed in the encircling gloom. Following Christ's admonition to teach all nations, Peter and Paul wisely set up the headquarters of their Church at the place where as the medieval proverb put it: *mille vie ducunt hominem per secula Romam* ('a thousand roads lead man forever towards Rome'). The spread of the faith was due as much to the existing imperial structures as to the efficacy of the preaching of the Early Fathers. Rome fell and Christianity became peripheral but these tough, homesick Irish *peregrini* who had been endowed with the gift of the faith brought it back again. By their dedication, resilience and if necessary obduracy they played a major part in making sure that there would eternally be a *spiritual* Rome to which all roads might lead.

GAZETTEER

(*Asterisks indicate separate entries.*)

Aachen

German city in North-Rhine Westphalia which has at different times in its history been French and Prussian. From the time of Charlemagne* until the Reformation, German emperors were crowned there and it was the centre of the Carolingian Renaissance. The *Gesta Karoli Magni* (*The Deeds of Charles the Great*), by the writer known as the Monk of Saint Gall, describes the arrival of Irish scholars offering wisdom: *si quis sapientiae cupidus est, veniat ad nos et accipiat eam!* ('If anyone wants wisdom, let him come to us and get it!') The *docti* in question were probably Clement Scottus* and Dungal* and, in answer to the emperor's question as to the price, they said, 'Suitable places, ready students and food and clothing without which our *peregrinationes* are impossible'.

Adomnán

Adomnán was born in Raphoe in 624, the son of Ronan and Ronnat, and probably received his early religious training locally. He went to Iona* in 652 and became abbot in 679. In 686 he visited Aldfrid, king of Northumbria, to sue for the release of Irish captives, and inspected the monasteries of Wearmouth* and Jarrow*. His acquaintance with the English church may have influenced his decision to accept the 'Roman' findings of the Synod of Whitby* (664). This did not endear him to the *Hibernenses* of Iona, and he returned to Ireland as a senior churchman with a mission to reconcile the Irish church to the Roman Easter. At the synod of Birr in 697 he sponsored canons (*Cáin Adamnáin*) for the protection of clergy, women and children, especially in time of war. He is also credited with the foundation of the monastery near his place of birth.

Adomnán is famous as the author of *Vita Columbae*, the life of his kinsman and founder of Iona, but he also wrote *De Locis Sanctis* (*On the Holy Places*) based on the observations of Bishop Arculf who had visited Palestine and other places in the Middle East. His name is associated with *Fís Adamnáin* (*Adomnán's Vision*), which is to be found in the twelfth-century *Lebor na hUidhre* (*The Book of the Dun Cow*). It describes a vision of heaven and hell rather like those of Fursa* and which also influenced Dante's *La Divina Commedia*. He died in 704 in an Iona which had not yet been reconciled to Roman rules.

AIDAN

The apostle of Northumbria was born in Ireland and educated at Senan's monastery on Scattery Island in the estuary of the Shannon. He was a monk of Iona and established himself on the tidal island of Lindisfarne* opposite Bamburgh, the residence of the Northumbrian kings, in 635. For more than a decade and a half he preached the Christian gospel and trained a native clergy. He founded churches, oratories and monasteries including Melrose* near

Galashiels in the border country of Lowland Scotland. His missionary work was encouraged by King Oswald, who became his interpreter to the English, having learned Irish during a period of exile on Iona*. (Oswald was martyred by the heathen Penda of Mercia (*c.* 577–655) in 642 and has been venerated since as a saint of the English church.) His successor and cousin Oswin (also a saint and martyr) continued his support of Aidan and the kingdom became Christian – and Celtic in its practices. When Oswin was murdered by his cousin Oswiu in 651, Aidan seemed to lose heart and died a fortnight later.

ALCUIN

Charlemagne*'s leading cultural advisor was born in York *c.* 737 and became master of the monastic school where he himself was trained. On his return from a visit to Rome in 781 he met the great emperor at Parma and accepted his invitation to come to the royal court at Aachen*. At first he supervised the education of the emperor's children but soon made the court a centre of intellectual and artistic activity – the so-called Carolingian Renaissance. Alcuin had been taught by Irish monks (he mentions a Colchu who may have been the abbot of Clonmacnoise) and he was responsible for bringing such *docti* to the palace school as Dungal*, Clement Scottus* and two other Irishmen, Joseph and Albinus. Dicuil*, Thomas and Cruinnmaol, all Irish, also played their part in the brief flowering of culture. In 796 Alcuin settled at Tours* as abbot and made it the premier school in the empire. While there he developed the 'Carolingian minuscule' calligraphy which he had learned at York from the Irish and which was to be the standard script for centuries. He kept in constant touch with Charlemagne by letter until his death in 804.

ALDHELM

The first English scholar of distinction received his early training from Maeldubh, the Irish founder of Malmesbury*. He was born in Wessex *c.* 640 and after his novitiate studied under Adrian and Theodore* at Canterbury. He returned to Malmesbury as abbot in 675 and in 705 was appointed bishop of Sherborne in Dorset. His education was an interesting combination of the Irish and the Roman traditions and he was the eighth-century equivalent of the modern media person: singing, dancing and telling jokes in the marketplace to attract the attention of the punters. His idea was to 'win men's ears – and then their souls'. His English writings, including the music of his songs and hymns, have been lost; extant in Latin are a treatise on virginity, written for the sisters of Barking convent in Essex, and a letter to Gerent, the king of Dumnonia (Devon and Cornwall) giving instructions for the calculation of the date of Easter according to the Roman way of reckoning and chiding his clerics through him for their adherence to Celtic practices. For relaxation he composed Latin verse, delighting in acrostics and other ingenious puzzles. He was a skilled architect and the little Anglo-Saxon church of Bradford-on-Avon in Wiltshire, discovered hidden in a jumble of other ecclesiastical buildings in 1856, is taken to have been designed by him.

Saint Aldhelm's Head, the promontory on the Dorset coast, south of Poole, commemorates him. He died in Dorset in 705 and his body was taken to Malmesbury for burial.

ANGOULÊME

Town on the Charente river in western France and an episcopal see that was run by two Irish bishops, Toimene (*fl.* 663–75) and Aillil, who died on 22 September 860.

ANNEGRAY

When Columban* obtained permission in 593 from the ruler of Austrasia* (probably Gunthram) to found his first monastery, he sought a place remote from men and conducive to prayer and mortification. He found it in the foothills of the Vosges mountains near the border of Burgundy. An old Roman fort served as the nucleus and the abbot found for himself a cave where he often subsisted on bilberries. The present-day village is eight miles east of Luxeuil* and recent excavations have revealed the foundations of the church, which was adapted from a temple of Diana, and some seventh-century sarcophagi.

ARIUS

Theologian born *c.* 250 in Ethiopia, the founder of the heresy known as Arianism. He was trained at Antioch and was a presbyter in Alexandria where he advanced the doctrine that Christ was not co-equal with God the Father but merely the highest of all finest beings, created by the Father by an act of free will. The heresy spread through the

Church in the Middle East but Arius was deposed and excommunicated in 321. To settle the controversy which rocked the whole Church and caused many deaths, inflicted by both its adherents and its enemies, the emperor Constantine called the Council of Nicaea in Bythinia in 325. Arius expounded his doctrine, to be refuted by Athanasius. Arius died in 336, poisoned, it was claimed by Arians, struck down by God according to the orthodox. The heresy was eventually suppressed in both the empires but it lingered in the German territories, longest in Lombardy where its greatest adversaries were Irish monks. It was finally eradicated by 662.

AUGUSTINE

Austin of Canterbury was prior of the Benedictine monastery of Saint Andrew in Rome when he was sent in 596 by Pope Saint Gregory the Great to preach the gospel to the heathen English. He landed in Thanet in 597 and was well received by King Ethelbert, whose wife Bertha was a Frankish Christian. After consecration as Archbishop of the English at Arles he set up his see at Canterbury where he founded the monastery of Saints Peter and Paul. His work of conversion was greatly helped when Ethelbert accepted baptism and before Augustine's death *c.* 605 he had established houses in London and Rochester as well. His missionfield was south-east England; when he tried to exert authority over the Celtic Christians in Wessex and Wales he was treated with suspicion in spite of a placatory synod which he held in west England at Aust on the Severn in 603. Gregory's interest was legendarily stimulated by seeing some tall blond handsome Angles offered for sale as slaves in the Roman Forum. He asked what nationality they were and being told said, '*Non Angli sed potius angeli.*' ('Not Angles but angels.')

AUSTRASIA

Originally the kingdom of Rheims, incorporating the basins of the Rhine, Moselle and Meuse rivers, with its capital at Metz*. The modern town is in Alsace-Lorraine and was part of the German empire 1871–1918. Its first king was the 'good' Merovingian Gunthram who welcomed Columban* in 593.

BEDE

Bede, known as 'venerable', was born near Monkwearmouth* in County Durham in 673. From the age of seven he lived in the monastery of Wearmouth* with its founder Benedict Biscop and went with him to his new foundation at Jarrow* in 884. He spent his whole life in Northumbria, devoting all his energies, as he put it, 'to the study of the Scriptures, observing monastic discipline and singing my daily services in church; study, teaching and writing have always been my delight.' He had a prodigious output of Biblical commentary, homilies, hymns, verse, martyrologies and the *Historia Ecclesastica Gentis Anglorum* (*Ecclesiastical History of the English People*) (731) which is a prime source for early English history and the lives of the Celtic saints in England. Though most of his writings are in Latin he was the first known writer of English prose. It is in the *Historia* that he wrote his famous analogy about the life of man:

> . . . quale cum te residente ad caenum, cum ducibus et ministris tuis tempore brumali . . . adveniens unus passerum domum citisse pervolaverit; qui cum per unum ostium ingrediens , mox per aliud exerit . . .
>
> (' . . . as if at wintertime when you sit feasting with your dukes and earls . . . a single sparrow might fly swiftly into the hall, coming in by one door and immediately flying out by another . . . ')

He died in 735 and was canonised in 1899 by Leo XIII.

BOBBIO

Town about fifty miles south of Milan which was the site of Columban*'s last monastery. It was founded in 612, three years before his death on 23 November 615. It, like many of the saint's other foundations, turned to the gentler Benedictine rule at an early stage of its history and lasted until its suppression by Napoleon in 1803. It was once famous for its library, the contents of which included the *Antiphonary of Bangor* and which are now scattered among many European libraries.

BREGENZ

Austrian town in the Vorarlberg province, beside the Bodensee

(Lake Constance) and close to the borders of Germany and Switzerland. It was Brigantium in Roman times and when Columban* paused there on his way to Italy it was in the territory of the Alemanni, a tribe of Germanic pagans. The location is very beautiful and this may have affected Columban's companion, Gall*, in his refusal to travel further. His illness which made him, as he thought, unfit to travel, could have been psychosomatic. Columban, his flinty religious superior, evidently thought so, since he placed on him the doom of never again saying Mass while he, Columban, lived. The arrival of his abbatial staff five years later, at the end of 615, was the sign that the doom was lifted and that Columbanus was dead. Gall and his rapidly acquired disciples had stayed about two years in Bregenz. As happened elsewhere, they settled upon an unused pagan temple that had been built on the site of an earlier Christian place of worship, in this case the chapel of Saint Aurelia. Gall is said to have broken up the infidel images and thrown them in the lake. This iconoclasm was followed by a blistering sermon in the Alemanni's own language, Gall still having a remarkable flair for alien tongues. The site may very well be near the *Gallusstein* ('Gall's Rock') in the Olrain area of the modern city of Bregenz.

Burgh Castle

Norfolk fortress, once the Roman *Gariannonum* and part of a chain of defences along the east coast of England. In the middle of the seventh century (*c.* 640), when it was known as Cnobheresburg, the ruins were adapted by Fursa*, his brothers, Foillan* and Ultan*, and his brothers in Christ, to the creating of an important Celtic monastery.

CADOC

Sixth-century founder of the monastery of Nant Carfan (later Llancarfan*) west of Cardiff. Known as 'Cadoc the Wise', his sphere of influence was the Celtic region on each side of the English Channel: in South Wales, Britanny and Cornwall. He was a contemporary and mentor of Gildas* who had a strong hand in shaping the form of Irish monasticism and numbered among his pupils Finnian* of Clonard. The stories about him are accounts of legendary marvels. He is said to have once been transported in a cloud from Llancarfan to Benevento in Italy. There he met a martyr's death after serving the see as bishop.

CANDIDA CASA

'White House' monastery, so called because it was built of white stone and not of wood as was customary. It was founded by Ninian* *c.* 400 on a cape called by its sixth-century Irish neophytes 'Rosnat' at Whithorn (or Whitern) near Wigtown in Galloway. As such it was conveniently placed for such alumni as Enda* of Aran and Finnian* of Moville and had an important influence on the course of Irish monasticism.

CANICE

Like his friend Comgall*, a Pict, Canice (Kenneth in Scotland) was born in north County Derry and became a pupil of Finnian* of Clonard. Like his contemporary Colum Cille* he spent some time at Glasnevin with Mobhi before going to work as a missionary in Scotland. Traditionally he was one of Colum Cille's companions on his journey to Inverness. He is taken to be the founder of the monasteries on Tiree, Coll, Mull and South Uist. He returned to Ireland towards the end of his life and established the monastery of Aghaboe. His name is memorialised in the city and county of Kilkenny. He died in 600.

CATHALD

Munster saint taken to be associated with Shanrathan, County Tipperary. (His uncorrupted robed body had *Cathaldus Rachau* engraved on a bishop's pectoral cross.) He was probably an abbot/bishop of Lismore, County Waterford, who went on pilgrimage to the Holy Land in 666. On his return he was invited to fill the vacant seat of Taranto*, (as happened to Donatus* in Fiesole*). He served until his death fifteen years later, having gained the reputation of a reforming and pious prelate. He is strongly venerated in Taranto, where a huge statue guards the port and a fresh water stream in the harbour is called *l'annello di San Cataldo* ('the ring of Saint Cathald') since it marks the spot where he is supposed to have stilled a storm by throwing his ring into the sea. He is the southern Italian patron of mariners, strong against shipwreck, and during World War II was patron of the Italian army.

Cedd

A seventh-century monk, born in Northumbria, and one of the native Anglo-Saxons who was trained by Aidan* at Lindisfarne*. He was sent *c.* 652 to evangelise the kingdom of Mercia and founded Lastingham Abbey in north Yorkshire. He became bishop of the East Saxons and founded many churches and monasteries before his death from plague in 664.

Chad

Brother of Cedd* and like him a pupil of Aidan* at Lindisfarne*. He succeeded his brother as abbot of Lastingham and thence went to York as bishop. Theodore* of Canterbury, the head of the English Church, who was bent upon establishing England as a fully ordered province of the Universal Church, challenged the legitimacy of his ordination. Chad humbly accepted the judgement and returned to Lastingham, thereby impressing Theodore with his obedience and character. Theodore soon appointed him bishop of the Mercians and established him at Lichfield *c.* 669. It was for a time a metropolitan see and a rival to Canterbury, its cathedral holding the relics of Chad until the Reformation. The present (now Anglican) cathedral, one of the small glories of English architecture, was begun in 1190 and took 150 years to build. Its most prized possession, the *Saint Chad Gospels*, is a manuscript book with the complete Matthew and Mark and part of Luke.

CHARLEMAGNE

Charles the Great (742–814) became king of the Franks in 771, king of the Lombards in 774 and first Holy Roman Emperor in 800, crowned so on Christmas Day by Leo III in gratitude for sweeping to rescue the pontiff from the rebellious Romans. Charlemagne ruled most of western Europe and was so noted as a lawgiver, administrator, protector of the Church and promoter of education that his court in Aachen* was the centre for an intellectual and artistic renaissance. He invited the greatest scholars of the day to take part in his work, the most notable being Alcuin* of York and the Irishmen, Clement Scottus*, Dicuil* and Dungal*. His special band of knights, called paladins, included Roland, who features in the famous eleventh century *Chanson*. Towards the end of his reign his northern territories were attacked by the Norsemen. He was succeeded by his son Louis the Pious (778–840), who continued Church reform but lacked his father's authority. During the latter's reign the old practice of subdivision between sons, probably necessary in the absence of the charismatic founder and to prevent dynastic strife, was resurrected. The portions assigned to heirs marked the remote beginnings of the modern countries of France, Germany and Italy.

Charlemagne was such a colossus in all aspects of kingship that he and his paladins figured in later romances of chivalry in which magical powers were ascribed to them. The legend of his readiness to reappear to lead the last battle against the Antichrist is shared by many other semi-mythical figures including King Arthur and Brian Boru.

Charles the Bald

Charles I (the Bald) was born in 823. He was the grandson of Charlemagne* and when his father, Louis the Pious, reverted to type and divided his empire between his sons, Charles received the Frankish territory that formed the nucleus of modern France. He had the same scholastic instincts as his great grandfather and set up schools which attracted scholars. Eriugena* was the doyen of the palace school at Laon*. Charles died in 877.

Clement Scottus

Irish scholar at the court of Charlemagne* after 791. He succeeded Alcuin* as chief scholastic. He had a perhaps unjustified reputation for arrogance; none of his writings is extant except a grammar *Ars Grammatica* (809–12) in which he lays stress on the universal use of Greek in his teaching. He died in Würzburg* and is buried in the cathedral crypt.

Colman

The third bishop of Lindisfarne* was Irish and like his predecessors a monk of Iona*. He became abbot in 661 on the death of the equally pro-Celtic Finan* and when Oswiu's decision went against him at the synod of Whitby* (664) stormed out, taking his Irish monks and thirty English colleagues with him back to Ireland, via Iona, where he did his best to confirm the community in adherence to the old ways. He set up a monastery on Inishbofin off the Galway coast but soon there was dissension in the community between the English monks and the others. (The Saxons claimed that all the farmwork was left to them). Colman organised a separate establishment on the mainland in Mayo for them and arranged for an English abbot, Gerald, to succeed him. The region was known after that time as *Muigheó na Sacsan*. Though on the opposite side in the authority controversy, Bede* is full of praise for the excellence of Colman's rule of Lindisfarne and its glory in his time.

COLUMBAN

Columban (also known by the Latin form of his name *Columbanus* and sometimes referred to as the 'the younger Columba') was born in south Leinster *c.* 543. As a handsome young man he was troubled by local girls, whom his first biographer called *lascivae puellae* ('lecherous wenches'), and on the advice of a local female hermit set his face against the world and followed the religious life. He studied with Sinell of Cleenish (on Lough Erne) and later with Comgall* at Bangor, a monastery famous even by the standards of the time for its austerity and learning. The tendency towards extreme asceticism never deserted him and the two rules that he devised for his monastic houses in Europe, *Regula Monachorum* (Monk's Rule) and *Regula Coenobialis* (Community Rule), reflected his own religious training. They impose regular fasting, broken by a meal of inferior quality late in the day, and give a list of graded punishments for offences – punishments which seemed so excessive that they were eventually rejected by the continental monks who gladly turned to the more benign rule of Benedict. Six slaps on the palm with a leather strap for coughing during the singing of a psalm or for celebrating Mass without a proper manicure was one of the lighter punishments.

Just as Colum Cille* had his hagiographer in Adomnán* so the greatest of the continental *peregrini* was memorialised by a monk who entered Bobbio*, the saint's last foundation, only three years after his death in 615. The *Vita* of Jonas of Susa* was published about 643 and though it has its necessary quota of miracles it is possible from it to follow Columban's adamantine career with some confidence in its veracity. (He had, it seems, power over wild animals, which was just as well considering that wolves and bears inhabited the woods and mountains where he sought privacy; he was remarkably delivered from prison; and he avoided banishment when the boat taking him from Nantes ran aground.) Jonas had the evidence of his subject's contemporaries, and was able to travel to Lake Constance to meet the saint's great companion Gall* and to visit the other Columban foundations.

Informal biographical material was also available to Jonas in Columban's own writings, some of which have come down to us intact. Any product of Bangor would be expected to be a good Latinist but Columban had a superior gift for literary composition, adding poetry to his sacred, epistolary and polemical writings. His *Carmen Navale*' ('Boat Song') was written to be chanted by monks as they fought their way up the 'two-horned Rhine', and 'To Fidolius' shows great linguistic ingenuity and gaiety. His writings show a thorough knowledge of the leading classical authors and Horace, with his moral comments on the vanity of artificial living, suited his temperament particularly. Even in his harangues he cannot help wordplay. In 614 he wrote to Pope Boniface IV (608–15) who, he feared, was yielding to heretical rulers as had Pope Vigilius (537–55) half a century earlier. The sentence: *Vigila itaque, quaeso, papa, vigila et iterum dico vigila, quia forte non bene vigilavit Vigilius* 'Be watchful, I urge you, Pope, be watchful and again I say be watchful, since perhaps he who was called Watchman did not watch well') is loaded with puns on the name of the previous pope. It is in this letter, too, written near the end of his life, that he mentions his home: *toti Iberi, ultimi habitatores mundi* . . . ('all of us Irish, denizens of the world's edge . . . ')

The letters, sermons, poetry and scriptural commentaries were all written by a man on the move, whose mission to preach was less vital than his need for solitude. He was in this respect the typical *peregrinus*, whose desire to live the religious life took precedence over everything else, whatever the cost in discomfort or even danger. He was well into his forties when he made his decision for exile and eventually wrung permission from Comgall to leave Bangor. He had twelve companions (a deliberate copy of Christ's pattern) including Gall, who was to quarrel with and separate from his leader. The intrepid band set out in 591 for what used to be the northern part of Roman Gaul but was now the land of the Franks and ruled by the notorious Merovingian dynasty that had been founded by Clovis (465–511) in 481. The territory was roughly that between the Loire and the Rhine but because of the tradition of subdivision there were both fraternal struggle and extension of rule. Though nominally Christian the area was largely pagan and the Christians were often followers of the heretic Arius*.

The activities of Clovis's grandchildren, Charibert, Chilperic, Sigebert and Gunthram, generated the kingdoms of Austrasia*. These included the north-east of France and west Germany and Neustria, which eventually was ruled from Paris and contained the land from modern Normandy south to Burgundy. The lives of these rulers, their actively conspiring consorts and their descendants were far from exemplary. There was much work for Columban and his companions to do. The first foundation was at Annegray* in the Vosges mountains. The Irishmen had been welcomed by the surviving grandson Gunthram and instinctively sought a site as remote as possible. They found it at a ruined temple of Diana which they converted to a church. Their reputation soon brought crowds of the faithful and, according to Jonas, miracles of healing were wrought and many young men joined the monastery.

Soon it was necessary to open a second house and the place chosen was Luxeuil*, eight miles to the west, where there were Roman ruins. This was to prove the premier monastery on French soil and its reputation brought so many neophytes that a third house was founded at Fontaine*, three miles to the north-west. By now Gunthram was dead and Columban found enemies in Gunthram's wife Brunhilde and son Theuderic, the new king. Theuderic had established a number of concubines in his palace who had produced four sons, and their grandmother required the stern Irish monk to give them his blessing. From what we know of the temper of Columban, it is clear that the moment must have been a tense one. Columban refused and relentless enmity resulted. Mother and son managed to set the local bishops against the Irish monks and their followers and a boycott resulted. Columban refused the king access to his cloisters and in 610 was ordered out of the kingdom.

The wanderer for Christ then became so literally. The band of monks, closely guarded by the king's soldiers, made a zig-zag progress across Neustria, from Luxeuil to Nantes by Besançon, Auxerre, Orleans and Tours. The boat that was to bring them to Ireland went aground and they managed, probably with the connivance of their escorts, to escape and make their way east again to Metz*, which was now the capital of Austrasia. Here the king Theudebert was friendly. He urged Columban and his band to preach the gospel in the south-eastern part of his kingdom. Columban decided to make for what is now Switzerland and establish Bregenz*, on the southeast shore of Lake Constance, the location of his newest monastery. The journey up the Rhine, often against fierce currents in the gorges between Bonn and Bingen, inspired the *Carmen Navale*. Bregenz, where the monastery was established, was an appropriate place to preach to the German tribe of the Alemanni who had never known Christianity.

In 612 the monks lost their royal patron, who was defeated and killed by his brother Theuderic, Columban's old enemy. The aging Columban (well into his seventies) was forced to move again, but at least he was on the path to Rome that seems to have been his dream. It was now that he and Gall parted at odds. Jonas's life, which removed all warts, draws a veil over the clash but Walafrid Strabo ('cross-eyed'), Gall's biographer, tells how Gall was stricken with an ague and pleaded that he was unfit to travel further. Columban, characteristically severe, would not accept this evidence of weakness and forbade him to say Mass for as long as he, Columban, should live.

The route south (suggested to the saint in a vision) lay through one of the Alpine passes to Lombardy. The monks reached Milan in 613. Agilulf, Duke of Lombardy, was an Arian but friendly, probably because his wife and children were true Christians. Columban accepted his hospitality but used his time in Milan to do most of his writings and preaching against Arianism. He was tiring and feeling his age – which was great considering the age-expectancy of the period – and he acquiesced in Agilulf's offer of a retreat at Bobbio. He died there on 23 November 613, having signified forgiveness to Gall by sending him his staff of office.

Such a life as Columban's, in its relentless mortification of body and mind, in its uncompromising courage and austere public defence of Christianity and in its relinquishing of what might have been an outstanding career in statesmanship, is hard for us to appreciate. He was conscious of his own tenderness and human weakness and may have assumed an external harshness as a carapace. He was no respecter of persons and his insistence on Celtic practices, especially about the dating of Easter, the relations between abbots and bishops and the tonsure, gave his clerical enemies a weapon against him. As we have seen his *regulae* proved too austere for later religious but he remains the great Irishman of Europe who relit the light that was not to be quenched.

COLUM CILLE

Ireland's 'first exile', the greatest and earliest of its missionaries, was born at Gartan in the heart of Tír Chonaill, probably on 7 December 521. His parents Feidlimid and Eithne were both of noble descent, the father belonging to the Cenél Conaill, a branch of the Uí Néill, and the mother a princess from Leinster. He was eventually named 'dove of the church' and given his early education by Cruithnechan, a Christian Pict who lived near Kilmacrenan, about eight miles from the birthplace. He became one of the pupils of Finnian of Clonard and elected to be ordained a priest.

Since he has held a special place in the imagination of the Irish through the centuries as the greatest of the native saints, he acquired a near-mythic status with an unusual accretion of tales of wonder-working and piquant anecdotes. These traditional stories, recorded in such works as the sixteenth-century *Betha Colaim Chille* by Maghnus Ó Domhnaill, have the advantage of suggesting the personality of the saint. We are lucky in that we have a biography written within a century of his death by a successor who, while mainly interested in the sanctity of his subject, gives excellent quotidian detail about his life and that of his companions. Adomnán*'s *Vita Columbae* was written not long after 688, when its author was in his sixties. The details of monastic life are, of course, those of Adomnán's time but it is reasonable to suppose that in such a conservative institution at such a time they reflect the conditions of Colum Cille's own day.

For seventeen years Colum Cille was engaged in study, preaching, teaching and copying. He is thought to have studied with Mobhí of Glasnevin and to have made scholastic visits to Enda* in Aran and Finnian* of Moville. The Irish foundations most prominently associated with his name are Derry and Durrow, but only the second can be shown definitely to have been founded personally by him and there is considerable argument about the date. The strong tradition that Derry was Colum Cille's first establishment (in 546) gave the city its name in Irish and made him its patron, but modern research indicates that it may have been set up by monks from his *paruchia* just as Kells, Swords, Drumcliffe and Tory were. (The word *paruchia,* which can mean 'parish' or 'diocese', usually signifies the total sphere of influence of a founding father.)

In 563 Colum Cille and twelve companions sailed to Iona* to establish a base for the conversion of the heathen part of Scotland. Adomnán gives Colum Cille's reason as a wish to be 'a pilgrim for Christ' and mentions the battle of Cúl Dreimne (561) as a handy means of dating the departure. The most famous of all the unauthenticatable (and most likely untrue) stories about the Donegal saint is that he was sent into exile as a penance for his involvement in an internecine struggle between the northern Uí Néill and the current *ard rí* Diarmait Mac Cerbaill that was settled with much bloodshed in the battle near Ben Bulben and cost 3,000 lives. The story may have its origin in Colum Cille's presence at the battle, for which he may very well have been drafted in by his aristocratic kinfolk as a kind of super army chaplain. Exile, though grievous, was preferable to endless involvement in politics. The many stories that have come down to us (including the famous judgement about the copied psalter) merely fill the vacuum left by the saint's adamant exit.

Iona is a small island south-west of the larger Mull about eighty miles north of County Antrim. In Colum Cille's time it lay within the Irish territory of Dál Riata, which was divided by the North Channel. Though Iona was sufficiently isolated to please even the most exacting anchorite, passage from the island to the many others that make up the inner and outer Hebrides and to the mainland was possible at most seasons. Using Iona as a base and with an instinct for politics that he now turned to the service of his mission, Colum Cille set up other foundations with the support not only of the Dál Riata but also of Pictish chieftains with whom he established good relations. Some authorities suggest that he founded thirty establishments in the islands and west coast, including monasteries on Hinba, Tiree and Skye. As with other aspects of the saint's life it is hard to separate the fancy from the fact. Since Scottish Dál Riata was at least nominally Christian it is most likely that the work of converting the Picts had already started before Colum Cille's arrival and the extent of his exclusive evangelisation may be exaggerated. The story of his journey up the Great Glen to Inverness, the stronghold of Brude, king of the northern Picts, is probably true, however. The two men seemed to have discovered a mutual liking and though Brude did not become a Christian he allowed missionary work in his realm to go unhindered.

As with other *peregrini* it is not possible to give precise reasons for Colum Cille's penitential leaving of the beloved country. Personal sanctification probably took precedence even over preaching the gospel. The monastic life was identical to that at home; work, mortification, prayer, and copying took up a large amount of the day. Though abbot, Colum Cille would have engaged in the same regimen as the merest postulant. He was known to be physically strong and had a lasting reputation as a penman. An eleventh-century poem put in his mouth mentions the 'ink of the green-skinned holly', and the belief that his is the hand that copied the fragment of the psalms preserved in the *Cathach* (*Battle Reliquary*) shows how persistent the tradition was. As well as miracles and visions his name is associated with prophecies (that he never uttered) but he almost certainly wrote Latin hymns including '*Altus Prosator*' ('Great Progenitor') and '*Noli, Pater*' ('Do not, Father').

Because of Colum Cille's position and temperament he was undoubtedly a major figure in the political life of Dál Riata, if not of Pictland. He certainly played kingmaker in 574 on the death of Gabhrán, king of Dál Riata, insisting that Aedán, the king's youngest son, be his father's heir, and his attendance at the important convention of Druim Cett near Limavady, County Derry, in 575, was as a senior authority on Dál Riata affairs. The assembly not only rationalised relations between the two parts of the territory but regularised at home the position of the *filid*, the learned class who combined poetry, oral history and genealogy. These were a pre-Christian survival, who had grown abusive and critical of the changed society. Colum Cille defended them against many critics and found for them a worthy place in the new dispensation. This strong support of the *filid* is traditionally ascribed to his early training by Gemman, who was a Christian bard. Certainly the eulogy *Amra Choluim Chille* ('Song of Colum Cille'), written by Dallán Forgaill ('chief of the poets of Ireland') on his death, is a tribute to a practitioner as well as a patron.

By the time the saint died in his seventy-seventh year, traditionally on Whit Sunday, 9 June 597, his work of preaching Christ to the Picts was well in hand. The monastery at Iona had become the supreme Christian centre in Scotland, and was as significant as any foundation in Ireland. Colum Cille's disciples, too, were to play an important part in the re-evangelising of Britain through the Columban foundations in Lindisfarne* and Whitby*. (That same summer Augustine* of Canterbury landed at Kent to begin this work.) Colum Cille represents the Celtic church better than any of his peers, in his steadfastness, energy, piety and humanity. He was the first to find that his vocation lay beyond the shores of Ireland. Others would follow and indeed travel much further but he had set a standard of achievement that would stay unchallenged. His remains are said to lie in Downpatrick, along with those of Patrick and Brigid, and there are many marvellous tales of how they arrived there. Perhaps, indeed, some relic of the saint was brought home at the time of the ninth-century evacuation of the abbey when the Book of Kells was preserved and one of many cherished stories of the saint is true. In a collection of Scots lore, *Carmina Gadelica*, he is known as *Chalum-Chille chaomh* ('Colum Cille the gentle'); from what we know of his fiery temperament that is the greatest tribute.

COMGALL

Abbot of Bangor, he was born in Antrim of Pictish extraction in 517 and was a soldier in his earlier career. He went to Scotland and lived on the island of Tiree, in one of the smaller monasteries founded from Iona*. He is believed to have gone with Colum Cille* and Canice* on his mission to Brude at Inverness. His great foundation at Bangor, established *c.* 555 on his return to Ireland, combined the austerity of Fintan's Cloonenagh with the dedication to learning of Finnian's Clonard. The remarkable *Antiphonary of Bangor,* created sometime between 680 and 691, which contains a long hymn in his founder's praise, is the monastery's glory, just as the *Book of Kells* is that of Iona. Among its famous alumni, apart from Columban*, are Gall*, Maelrubha*, Moluag and Malachy (1094–1148) who became the great reforming archbishop of Armagh. Comgall died at Bangor in 603.

CRUINDMEL

Irish *doctus* who lived in some part of the Frankish empire in the first half of the ninth century. His treatise on scansion and metrication is important because of the many examples he quotes from classical and early Christian writers. He used

Bede*'s *De Metrica Arte* as his chief source and his work contains excerpts by diverse authorities, from Virgil and Horace to Aldhelm* and Donatus*.

CUMMIAN OF BOBBIO

Irish saint known only from an epitaph found in the monastery of Bobbio*. His name was Cummianus and his memorial stone was erected by a Lombardy duke called Liutprand who reigned 712–44. According to the inscription, Cummian spent the last seventeen years of his life there as bishop and died at an advanced age.

CUTHBERT

Bishop of Lindisfarne* (who may have been Irish in spite of his English name) born *c.* 634 and appointed to Holy Island in 684 after serving at Melrose* under Eata*. Like the young Patrick he herded sheep as a boy and is credited by Bede* with having had a vision in which he saw angels conveying Aidan*'s soul to Paradise. He was a tireless traveller, preacher and administrator and notable for his efforts to heal the monastic rift left by the dissension at Whitby. Like any Irish monk he preferred to have solitude to pray and serve God; this he found on Farne to which he regularly resorted and where he died in 687.

DICUIL

Little is known about his life except what can be gathered from his writings. He was Irish and had a teacher called Suibne (an Ulster name). He met in 767 a monk called

Fidelis who had visited the Holy Land and was able to give him reasonably accurate knowledge about Egypt and the Nile. The teacher is almost certainly the abbot of Iona* who died in 772. Dicuil went to the continent *c.* 806, probably to escape Viking attacks, and became a teacher at the palace school of Charlemagne* at Aachen*. He died *c.* 825. He is famous as an early geographer and astronomer. His great work, *Liber de Mensura Orbis Terrae* (*The Book of Measurement of the Earth*) was presented shortly before his death. The title shows that geography did not exist as a separate subject but, like astronomy, was subsumed under geometry (literally 'earth-measuring'). Dicuil's detailed account of the Scottish Isles as far north as the Faroes suggests personal knowledge and he was aware of Iceland's inshore waters being ice-free all year round. He had obtained this information from venturesome Irish monks who also told him about the midnight sun. Scholars believe he was the anonymous Irish poet who wrote a verse tribute to Charlemagne under the pseudonym *Hibernicus Exul* ('Irish Exile').

DONATUS

Ninth-century Irish bishop of Fiesole, the Etruscan town in the hills above modern Florence. He was returning to France from a pilgrimage to Rome in 829 at a time when the see was vacant and his coming was seen as a sign from heaven. He ruled as bishop until 876 and in that time wrote much poetry including a verse life of Saint Brigid and a description in Latin of his homeland. Columban's monastery of Bobbio* was in his diocese and he is recorded as giving the church and hospice called Saint Brigid's at Piacenza into the monastery's keeping in 850.

DONNAN

A monk of Iona who founded *c.* 600 a monastery on Eigg*. At Easter 617 he and fifty other monks were massacred by 'sea-rovers'. These were probably Scandinavian and may have been a hit-squad hired by local Picts to show their disapproval of the Irish. (According to tradition it was a local chieftainess who disapproved of holy men on her islands who arranged it.) The monks, it is said, were herded into the refectory and the building was set on fire. Donnan is venerated throughout western Scotland and he has given his name to the castled island Eilean Donan in Loch Alsh.

DROSTAN

A disciple of Colum Cille*, he was appointed abbot of Deer, in northeast Aberdeen, traditionally the last monastery founded by the saint. It survived as a Celtic monastery until the thirteenth century, when as New Deer it became Cistercian. The ninth-century *Book of Deer* has much Irish material interpolated in the twelfth century, proof of its Celtic character.

DUNGAL

Carolingian scholar who came from Ireland about 784 and lived as a recluse at Saint Denis*, near Paris. After an eclipse of the sun in 810 he was invited by the emperor to explain it. His letter, though still using the Ptolemaic system (with the earth as the fixed centre), shows independent astronomical observation. Either he or another Irishman of the same name was in northern Italy in the 820s. This man was made supervisor of education in the region by Lothair II, the grandson of Charlemagne*, who was granted Italy and the title Holy Roman Emperor by his father Louis the Pious. He was a kind of inspector general to whom the scholars of other schools had to come for what we would now call refresher courses. He left his library to the Columban abbey of Bobbio* where he ended his days and since it included a copy of the *Antiphonary of Bangor* it is assumed that like the founder he was a pupil of Comgall*.

DUNKELD

Site on the River Tay about sixteen miles north of Perth that was chosen by Kenneth MacAlpin, who reigned from 847 to 858 as the first king of a united Scotland, to be the kingdom's primatial see, thereby diminishing the authority of Iona*. A previous monastery had been destroyed by Vikings, who found the upper waters of the Tay as navigable as those of the Shannon. Kenneth I restored the foundation and conveyed the remaining relics of Colum Cille* there. The move effectively separated the Scots and Irish churches, though Irish monks continued to worship there and receive novices from Ireland. By the twelfth century the Columban monks were replaced by secular canons. Dunkeld continued as an episcopal see and is still a diocese of the Scottish Catholic Church.

EATA

Abbot of Melrose* who in spite of his strong support of the *Hibernenses** at Whitby* became bishop of Lindisfarne* after Colman*. He had been one of Aidan*'s first neophytes when the monastery on Holy Island was founded and, recognising the sanctity and diplomacy of his pupil Cuthbert*, whom he had left at Melrose, changed places with him and allowed him to continue with the task of reconciliation after Whitby.

EIGG

Island between Mull and Skye about fifty miles north of the former, the site of the destruction of Donnan's monastery and the massacre of the monks on Easter Sunday 617 by what was probably an early, water-testing Viking raid.

ENDA

Like Comgall*, he gave up a military career for the monastic life and did his novitiate in *Candida Casa** under Ninian*. In no sense a rival to Finnian's Clonard* his monastery (traditionally the first to be established in Ireland) on Inis Mór, the largest of the Aran Islands in Galway Bay, was noted for the severity of its rule. Mortification had precedence over learning and it was often a place of spiritual retreat for other monks. He died in his monastery *c.* 530.

ERIUGENA

John Scottus Eriugena, named Irish (*Scottus*) in Latin and Greek, was born *c.* 810 and reached maturity when the Viking raids in Ireland were at their most virulent. By the early 840s he was at the court of Charles the Bald* (823–77), the grandson of Charlemagne* who is taken to be the first king of France. He, although to a smaller extent than his great grandsire, encouraged scholars, and Eriugena was employed by the king as master of the court school and as a translator of theological works into Latin. It was at Laon*, one of Charles's palaces, that he wrote in 851 his famous treatise *De Praedestinatione*, intended by his clerical patron Bishop Hincmar as an answer to the heretical views of the imprisoned Augustinian theologian Gottschalk, whose work, which denied not only predestination but the existence of evil itself, was condemned at the Council of Valence in 855.

Eriugena's greatest work, *Peri Pheusis* (in Latin *De Divisione Naturae*), written in 867, takes the popular form of dialogue between pupil and master. It was condemned as pantheistic in 1225 and put on the *Index* of prohibited books in 1685. It is only since the beginning of this century that his views are considered tenable by Christians. His translation, commissioned by Charles, of the Neo-platonist disquisition known as the *Pseudo-Dionysius* had a profound effect on medieval thought and prepared the way for modern metaphysics. The excellence of the translation caused one critic to express surprise that a barbarian from the ends of the earth should have been such a master of Greek. Like all great personalities, Eriugena attracted a number of legends: one such, that on Charles's death in 877, he went to teach in Alfred's Wessex as abbot of Malmesbury*, may be true but the macabre tailpiece that he was stabbed to death by the pens of his pupils is probably a piece of student wishful thinking. Another records what has been called the greatest *bon mot* of the Middle Ages. Once at table the king, Charles the Bald, asked him '*Quid distat, Scottum et sotum*?' ('What is the difference between an Irishman and a drunkard?') and got the answer: *Tabula tantum!* ('Just the table!'). He probably died in France in 877.

FERGAL *SEE* VIRGIL

FIACHRA

Seventh century Irish hermit who accidentally gave his name to the French four-wheeled cab. (The *fiacres* first made their appearance in the streets of Paris in 1620 and had their stand outside the Hôtel Saint-Fiacre.) He is traditionally the one said to have brought the last sacraments to Comgall* and to have brought the embalmed arm of the saint to his monastery at Ullard in County Kilkenny, where there are still remains. On his arrival in France *c.* 650 he was received kindly by Bishop Faro of Meaux* in Neustria (the region now famous for Brie cheese) and set up an eremitical cell at Brieux. He was probably the first to establish a hospice for Irish travellers, both scholarly travellers and those on pilgrimage. The modern town of Saint-Fiacre-en-Brie is built on the site of the original hospice which was strictly for men. Later many more hospices were built, with similar guesthouses provided in nunneries for women. Fiachra's reputation for sanctity and miraculous cures long outlived him (he died in 670) and he was greatly venerated throughout Europe in the Middle Ages. His cell and shrine (at Meaux) were places of pilgrimage, especially by sufferers from syphilis. He is also the patron saint of gardeners because of the excellence of the vegetables he grew about his hermitage.

FIESOLE

Town noted for its Etruscan remains, four miles north of Florence. It was the bishopric of the Irish saint Donatus* from 829 to 876. His head, enclosed in a bust of gilt bronze, is in the church of San Domenico, the village half-way between the town and Florence.

FINAN

Aidan*'s successor at Lindisfarne*. Like him he was an Irish monk of Iona* and succeeded in baptising not only Peada, the son of the unregenerate pagan Penda, but also Oswiu, who had killed Oswin (and Penda), Aidan's second patron. He carried on the missionary work, bringing the faith with a Celtic flavour into the lands south of the Humber. He strongly resisted pressure from the English Church to accept the Roman instructions about the date of Easter, the monastic tonsure and the other elements of divergence between the Celtic and the Universal Church. He died in 661, three years before the Whitby* synod which ruled against the Irish practices.

FINDAN

Irishman (also known as Fintan) who was captured as a slave from a Leinster abbey by Vikings and carried off to the Orkneys. He escaped and in thanksgiving went on pilgrimage to Rome. On his return home, he stopped off at a small monastic settlement on an island called Reinau in the Rhine near the Swiss town of Schaffhausen, on the border with Germany. He spent four years in normal monastic duties and then the remaining twenty-two years of his life as a recluse. He died in 878.

FINNIAN OF CLONARD

The father of Irish monasticism, he was trained at Cadoc*'s monastery at Llancarfan* where he was a friend and fellow-pupil of Gildas*. His monastery at Clonard (in present-day County Westmeath) was where he trained the so-called 'Twelve Apostles of Ireland': Ciaran of Saiger, Ciaran of Clonmacnoise, Brendan of Clonfert, Brendan of Birr, Colum Cille*, Colman of Terryglass, Molaise of Devenish, Canice of Aghaboe, Riadan of Lorrha, Mobhi of Glasnevin, Sinell of Cleenish and Ninidh of Inishmacsaint. Like his Welsh masters he emphasised the pre-eminence of study and he urged his leading pupils to leave and set up their own foundations. Though he was personally ascetic his rule was less austere than that of Enda*. He died of plague in 549.

FOILLAN

One of the brothers of Fursa*, who left Ireland to escape the adulation that his sermons had created and with him helped to establish Burgh Castle*. When Fursa left for France, Foillan became abbot but as the kingdom of East Anglia was attacked by the pagan Mercians he followed Fursa. Mayor Pepin of Landen (whose wife Itta had already founded a nunnery at Nivelles* in modern Belgium with her daughter Gertrude as abbess) gave him land at Fosses. The two establishments kept close ties with each other and it was on a journey from Nivelles to Fosses that Foillan met his death in 665, murdered by robbers in the forest of Seneffe.

Fontaine

The third monastery founded in Austrasia* by Columban* because of the great popularity, both among postulants and among pilgrims, of Annegray* and Luxeuil*. It lies three miles north-west of the latter. Columban moved freely between the three houses until his expulsion by Theuderic in 610.

Fridian

Irish founder of a monastery at Lucca*, who became bishop there in 560 and was noted for his struggles with the Arian heresy. He died on 18 March 588 and his relics, reconstituted in wax, are in a glass coffin in the church that bears his name. He is credited with miraculously changing the course of the river Auser, which once was a tributary of the Arno but now flows directly into the Ligurian Sea.

Fursa

After Columban* Fursa (also called Fursey) is the best known of the Irish missioners in Europe. He gained such a reputation as a preacher in Ireland that he decided in Bede*'s words: 'to go on pilgrimage for the Lord wherever opportunity offered'. He came to England with his brothers

Foillan* and Ultan* sometime after 630 and was welcomed by King Sigebert of East Anglia. He established the monastery of Cnobheresburgh (now Burgh Castle* near Yarmouth in Suffolk) and ministered there for ten years. Then, inspired by the work of Columban*, he left for France. Erchinoald, the mayor of the palace* in Neustria*, became his patron and gave him land to found a house at Lagny near Paris about the year 644. When he died at Mézerolles on his way back to England in 648 his uncorrupted body was brought by the mayor to be the centrepiece of the new church he had completed at Péronne*. His accounts of visions of the world of the spirits, both good and evil, of the fires of sin ready to consume the earth and of the joyous state of the blessed brought him lasting fame and influenced a deal of religious thought in medieval Europe. He is one of the main sources of Dante's *Divine Comedy*.

GALL

Gall was born *c.* 550 and was a student of Columban* at Bangor before going as one of his twelve companions to the land of the Franks in 591. He was still in his company and particularly useful because of his linguistic ability when Columban established the monastery in Bregenz on Lake Constance in 612. The story that he and his master quarrelled there when Columban accused him of malingering is not included in Jonas*s life of the saint, but Gall's biographer Walafrid Strabo records that Columban said to his friend, who had been stricken with a fever: 'I enjoin on you before I go, that so long as I live in the body, you do not dare to celebrate Mass . . . ' (That story concludes with the arrival of Columban's abbatial staff five years later, sent by the dying monk to release Gall from the interdict.) Gall, quickly picking up the local patois, stayed to preach to the Alemanni, a German tribe that had never been Christian, with the approval of Duke Gunze and other local rulers. He is traditionally known as a successful angler and he probably chose the site of his cell, by the upper waters of the Steinach river, deliberately. He is said to have attracted the significant twelve disciples to this hermitage and to have practised the same austerity of living as that imposed by Columban. By the time of his death in 640 he and his monks had converted the territory that is now Switzerland. The monastery and town of Sankt Gallen* (founded by the Benedictine Otmar in 719) are his lasting tribute.

GILDAS

Like his contemporary Cadoc, called 'the Wise'. He was born a Pict *c.* 493 in the Clyde valley of Scotland but left the place because of the strife that reigned there. Settling in Wales he married, but became a monk after the death of his wife. He studied under Illtud* at Caldey Island and received a good education. His book *De Excidio et Conquestu Britanniae* ('On the Ruin and Conquest of Britain'), written between the years 516 and 547, is the only extant history of the Celts and the only contemporary account of Britain from the time of Caesar's invasion. It concludes with a violent denunciation of the kings, clergy and people of Gildas's own time. Gildas stayed for a period in isolation on an island in the Bristol Channel but clearly visited Ireland, since his influence on the Irish church, especially through Clonard, was considerable. His later life, according to a strong Breton tradition, was spent in Britanny, where he founded a monastery at Rhuys. He died on the island of Houat in Quiberon Bay *c.* 570.

GLASTONBURY

One of the oldest archaeological sites in England, noted for its tor (topped by a fourteenth-century church tower), associated with King Arthur and also with the legend that Joseph of Arimathea buried the Holy Grail, the chalice used at the Last Supper, there. At the time of the Crucifixion it would have been a lake isle and it is taken to be the site of Avalon where Arthur lies sleeping. In about 688 King Ine of Wessex – who reigned until 726 and after abdication died on a pilgrimage to Rome – founded a monastery there which was manned by Irish monks. William of Malmesbury* wrote some of his histories in Glastonbury and an interpolation by an anonymous hand claims that Patrick of Ireland resided there for a time. Later the monks insisted that the apostle was buried there. It was a popular place of pilgrimage for the travelling Irish, particularly during the reign of Alfred the Great (871–899) who received them hospitably at his court.

ILLTUD

Fifth-century abbot (*c.* 425–505) who founded Llantwit monastery in Glamorgan and Ynys Byr on Caldey Island off the south Wales coast. The rule of both these foundations placed great stress on learning and study and less on manual labour. His disciples Cadoc* and Gildas* all played their parts in the development of Irish monasticism.

IONA

The rocky island in the Inner Hebrides off the southwest head of Mull which Colum Cille* made his centre for the evangelising of pagan Pictland (Scotland) in 563. The original Gaelic name was *I* which means 'island' and it is thought that 'Iona' was a misreading by a copyist of Adomnán's Latin version *Iova insula*. Iona is 3.5 miles long by 1.5 miles at its widest and, significantly, Ireland is not visible from it, though the coast of Antrim is only eighty miles away. Of its 2,000 acres, about 500 are arable. Its (probably few) aboriginal inhabitants were Scots-Irish of Dál Riata, who even then treated the North Channel as a large territorial lake, not much wider than Lough Neagh, if much stormier. The island traditionally was the burial ground of Dalriadan kings who were interred in *Reilic Odhráin*, dedicated to a saint who had died in 549. It was beside this graveyard that Colum Cille built his monastery. His cell, by custom somewhat bigger and set apart, is thought to have been set on Tor Abb. The pattern was exactly that of such compounds at home in Ireland. There would have been a monastery church, a refectory with a kitchen, a library and *scriptorium* (which saw the beginnings of the great *Book of Kells*), workshops, stores and necessary offices and a *hospitium* ('guest house') which soon became one of the most used buildings because of the fame of the establishment.

Soon it was necessary to expand, and similar compounds were established on the islands of Coll and Tiree, which lay west of northern Mull. Colum Cille typically needed to follow the *peregrinus*'s desire for solitude and regularly took himself off to the island of Hinba, which is known in modern Scots Gaelic as *Eileach an Naoimh* ('Saint's Rock'). It is indeed little more than a granite plug that lies in the Firth of Lorne, halfway between Mull and Jura to the south and about seven miles from each. The waters of Argyllshire are subject to severe westerly gales for most of the year but the Inner Hebrides at least form a kind of giant's causeway which allows relatively safe island-hopping.

Iona's *hospitium* had soon to deal with many visitors, mainly pilgrims, though students and novices flocked to be part of the community of the Irish exile. Other visitors came on political missions, since Colum Cille and his senior monks were sources of authority and wisdom. The Dál Riata kings and later the Pictish rulers brought their quarrels for arbitration and the abbot, well-experienced in the politics of the time, had the authority of aristocracy in his own personality. Relations with local rulers were not always peaceful, as the fate of Donnan* of Eigg* demonstrates, but the abbots who succeeded Colum Cille, usually kinsmen, combined lay and ecclesiastical authority as primates of the region. This they exercised with integrity but not always with diplomacy. *I* remained for centuries a centre of the Irish church and a powerhouse of evangelisation. Its success in northern England was spectacular: alumni of Iona and the disciples they trained overcame the German paganism that had been the condition of England since the middle of the sixth century. Aidan's Lindisfarne* became the Iona of Northumbria and generated English monasteries in the manner of the Pictland centre. The loyalty of Iona's monks to Ireland and the founder led them to near-schism when the Celtic Christianity that they preached seemed to be contrary to the teaching of Rome. The Iona-generated communities held out for a long time against the edicts of Whitby*, even to the extent of rejecting the spiritual advice of one of their own abbots. Adomnán*, the ninth abbot (679–704) and biographer of Colum Cille, had become convinced of the need for obedience to Rome even in such relatively trivial matters as had caused the dissension, but his advice was rejected. He left for Ulster, where his mission to bring about obedience to Rome was successful. It was not until twelve years after his death in 704 that Iona finally conformed.

Iona continued to be a premier Irish monastery until the second wave of northern barbarians undid the work of three hundred years of civilisation. The first Vikings appeared in 795, to raid an Iona defenceless against a sea attack. They pillaged and killed and carried off slaves; they returned in 802 and again in 806 when they killed sixty-eight monks. In 814 Ceallach the abbot decided on flight, and returned to Ireland, bearing the precious relics of Colum Cille and the unfinished *Book of Kells*. Iona survived further Viking attacks and remained an Irish monastery until the beginning of the thirteenth century. At this point, it was replaced by a Benedictine Abbey which survived until the sixteenth century. More significant than the twentieth-century archaeological discoveries, which confirm long-held traditions, is the spirit of Iona, which is one of the glories not only of the Irish Church but of western civilisation. Only its difficulty of access, not much easier now than in Colum Cille's time, prevented its taking its place with Rome, Compostella and Canterbury as an honoured place of pilgrimage.

JARROW AND MONKWEARMOUTH

Northumbrian monasteries founded by Benedict Biscop (*c.* 628–*c.* 690), the assistant of Theodore* of Canterbury. Modern Wearmouth was established in 674 and Jarrow eight years later. Abbot Benedict exercised his considerable influence to make them as grand as the Celtic Lindisfarne, using regular visits to Rome to bring back relics, sacred images, stonemasons, glaziers and even the precentor of Saint Peter's to teach his choristers the Roman fashion of plainchant. He was assiduous in building up the libraries, thus making possible the literary work of the foundation's most famous denizen, Bede*.

JONAS

Biographer of Columban* who was born in Susa in the Piedmont alps *c.* 600 and entered the monastery of Bobbio* in 618. It was the last foundation of his subject who had died only three years before. Jonas was thus able to talk to witnesses who had known the saint intimately, including

Gall* with whom Columban had clashed over obedience. Jonas, a scholar in his own right, became secretary to a succession of abbots of Bobbio and in travels with them garnered much information about the saint's life. The travels were extensive and it was not until the years 640–2 that he settled to write his *Vita Columbani*. (*Life of Columban*). It is a reliable document if one ignores the stories of miracles that were a necessary part of such exemplary lives.

KILIAN

Seventh-century saint from Mullagh in County Cavan who preached Christianity to the Thuringians and the Franconians. One of his converts was Duke Gozbert whom he persuaded to abandon his wife, Geilana, who had been his brother's wife. She is supposed to have had Kilian and some fellow missionaries murdered. His body was buried in the crypt of Würzburg* cathedral which bears his name.

KÖLN (COLOGNE)

Largest city of west Germany. Site of the 'Irish' monastery of Saint Martin the Great which flourished in the eleventh and twelfth centuries. Its most famous *doctus* was Marianus Scottus* (Mael Brígte from Moville on Strangford Lough).

LAON

Town in France seventy-five miles northeast of Paris. It was the seat of one of the palace schools of Charles the Bald*, noted especially for the presence of John Scottus Eriugena.

LIÈGE

Belgian city, cultural centre of the French-speaking part of the country, where Sedulius Scottus* ran the cathedral school.

LINDISFARNE

Known nowadays as Holy Island, the cradle of English Christianity lies at the end of a three-mile causeway, which allows access during a six-hour period between tides. The place was an ideal location for a Celtic monastery and when Aidan* came from Iona* in 635 at the invitation of Oswald, the Christian king of Northumbria, he made it the centre of his mission. By 664 it was a well-established monastery and the mother house of several others, including Melrose*, Hartlepool, Coldingham, Tadcaster and Lichfield. It could be described as the Iona of the northeast, the dynamic centre for the rechristianising of England and much more influential than Augustine*'s foundations in Kent. A later bishop, Cuthbert*, who may in spite of his Anglo-Saxon name have been Irish and was certainly trained by Irish monks, became abbot in 664, when Colman* in an irreconcilable quarrel over the findings of the Synod of Whitby* led the Irish monks and thirty Anglo-Saxon ones away. Under Cuthbert, the great Lindisfarne craft of illuminated manuscripts which combined Celtic and continental design was developed. It is likely that the *Book of Durrow* (late seventh century) originated there and, like the later *Book of Kells*, was brought to Ireland for safekeeping when coastal sites like Iona and Lindisfarne were the object of Viking raids. The *Lindisfarne*

Gospels (*c.* 700) are the authenticated glory of Aidan's settlement.

LLANCARFAN

Early sixth-century foundation of Cadoc* the Wise, situated west of modern Cardiff. Finnian* of Clonard, one of the great shapers of Irish monasticism, was one of its alumni and its links with Clonard were strong. Its monks was eligible for election as abbot of Clonard and it held lands along the Liffey. It was here that Finnian learned the value of study as an appropriate part of the monastic life.

LUCCA

Town in Tuscany and site of pre-Roman Etruscan town twelve miles from Pisa, whose patron is Fridian*.

LUXEUIL

Site of Columban*'s most famous monastery founded *c.* 590. The town lies 230 miles south-east of Paris, its modern name Luxeuil-les-Bains. It was one of the great mother houses of European monasticism. The abbey later adopted the Benedictine rule and survived until the French Revolution. The monastic buildings have been incorporated into a seminary and the church was granted the status of basilica in 1926.

MAELRUBHA

Founder of the monastery of Applecross, in Ross, near Skye, he was a monk of Bangor and laboured in the northern parts of Pictland for nearly fifty years (673–722). His name is remembered in Loch Maree and there are relics of his work to be found in Sutherland and Banff.

MALMESBURY

Town in Wiltshire, near Swindon, site of a seventh-century abbey founded by Maeldubh, a learned monk from Ireland. His more famous pupil, Aldhelm*, took charge of the monastic school *c.* 675. William of Malmesbury (*c.* 1090–*c.* 1143), the first significant English historian after Bede*, was a monk there. His main works are *Gesta Regum Anglorum* (*Deeds of English Kings*) which told the known history of England from 449 to 1120, *Gesta Pontificum Anglorum* (*Deeds of English Pontiffs*) which covered ecclesiastical history from 597 to 1125 and *Historia Novella* (*New History*) which covered the years 1128–42 and which was left unfinished at his death. He lived for some time at Glastonbury*, another Irish foundation about sixty miles away in Somerset. His writings contain useful information on the Irish *peregrini*. He is the source of the anecdotes about Eriugena* and suggests that Eriugena was abbot of Malmesbury before his death.

MARIANUS SCOTTUS (OF COLOGNE)

Máel Brigte was born in 1028 and entered the monastery of Moville in Strangford Lough in 1052. Four years later the abbot, Tighernach Bairrcec, sentenced him to exile for a reason now unknown. Máel Brigte arrived at Cologne and stayed as a Benedictine monk in Saint Martin's until 1058.

Then he left for Fulda and upon ordination a year later had himself walled up as an incluse. Ten years later he moved to a similar position in Mainz*. His great work, *Chronicon Universale*, tells the story of the world from the Creation to 1082. It includes a great deal of Irish ecclesiastical history and is particularly good on the Irish scholars of his time. Máel Brigte died in 1082 or 1083.

MARIANUS SCOTTUS (OF RATISBON)

Muiredach Macc Robartaig was born in Donegal and left on pilgrimage for Rome in 1067. He stayed for a year at the monastery of Michelsberg in Bamberg before going on to Ratisbon (Regensburg)*. He and his companions were presented with the church of Weih Sankt Peter. As the numbers of the Irish community increased, they built the larger monastery of Saint James which was opened in 1111. It became the mother house of a number of Benedictine foundations in Germany and Austria that were known as the *Schottenklöster** ('Irish monasteries') and that also had two houses at Rosscarbery and Cashel. Muiredach died in 1088.

MAYORS OF THE PALACE

Stewards of the later Merovingian kings who gradually obtained power due to the lack of activity on the part of the sovereigns.

MEAUX

Town north-east of Paris and centre of the Brie cheese industry. It was the see of Bishop Faro (d. 672) to which he welcomed two Irish monks in the mid-seventh century. Fiachra* led a hermit's life in Breuil. Kilian went to Aubigny where he is still venerated. Like Eriugena*, Aldhelm* and Martinus Hiberniensis*, he was an associate of Charles the Bald*'s palace school at Laon*.

MELK

Austrian town about forty miles west of Vienna with a Benedictine abbey set on a fortified crag overlooking the Danube. It is connected with Colman, the son of the Irish *ard rí* Maolsheachlainn II, who on a pilgrimage to Rome in 1012 was tortured and hanged at a place called Stockerau. When miracles were associated with his corpse the remains were taken by the local ruler Henry I to his stronghold at Melk. His son, Emperor Henry II (1002-24), built an ornate tomb to house the relics and the place became a regular place of call for Irish pilgrims. There are many churches dedicated to Colman throughout Austria, Hungary and southern Germany. In the last area Colman is a popular baptismal name. Colman is also prayed to on his feast day by women in search of husbands.

MELROSE

Abbey in Selkirk near Galashiels in the Scots borders country founded from Lindisfarne* *c.* 640. Eata*, the first abbot, was a Northumbrian pupil of Aidan*. It was the school of Cuthbert*, whose life and work resembled Patrick of Ireland. In 1136 it became the site of the first Cistercian house in Scotland and survived until the sixteenth-century suppression.

Merovingian Dynasty

A dynasty of Frankish kings that flourished from the fifth century until 751, when the last king Childeric III was deposed by Pepin the Short*. The name of the dynasty came from the semi-mythical Merovech but the first powerful king was Clovis (465-511). His decision to divide his territory between his four sons was an invitation to fratricide, although the Merovingian territory was greatly extended. Nominally Christian, the Merovingians were on the whole not antagonistic to the Irish *peregrini*. Though classical learning was eclipsed in their time and lawlessness was endemic in their territories, their architecture was neo-classical and the bell tower their contribution to ecclesiastical architecture. In time, real power fell into the hands of their major-domos, the Mayors of the Palace*.

Metz

French city on the Moselle which was the Merovingian capital of Austrasia* in the sixth century. Its abbey of Saint Clement had two Irish abbots in succession in the tenth century when it was the centre of necessary monastic reform. The first, Cadroe, was appointed *c.* 953 and reigned there until his death in 978. Fingen, who succeeded him, was also abbot of Symphorian in the district. He died in 1004.

Moluag

A Pict from Dál Riata, an alumnus of Bangor and a

contemporary of Maelrubha*, he set up a monastery on the shores of Loch Linnhe in Argyll.

NEUSTRIA

The western kingdom that was carved out of the realm of Clovis (465–511), the Merovingian king, and eventually ruled by his grandson Charibert (561–575). It comprised modern Normandy and lands to the south and east, having Paris as its capital.

NINIAN

British bishop who was educated in Rome and set up in 400 the famous monastery called *Candida Casa** at Whithorn on the Solway Firth (traditionally his birth region) as a centre for evangelising the pagan Picts. He is believed to have visited (at Tours) Saint Martin, the father of monasticism in Gaul and to have followed his ideas.

NIVELLES

Belgian town twenty miles south of Brussels, site of monastery founded by Foillan* for Irish monks in 652. The relics of the saint, who was slain by robbers near Fosses in 655, are paraded every seven years in *La Marche de Saint Feuillen*.

NÜRNBERG

Bavarian city, once the shrine of Nazism and location of the war crimes trials. It was the site of a *Schottenkloster* which was founded in 1140.

PEPIN THE SHORT

Mayor of Neustria and Burgundy (*c.* 715–768), son of Charles 'Martel', the 'hammer of the Saracens', who dethroned Childeric III, the last of the Merovingian kings in 751. He founded the Carolingian dynasty of which the most outstanding member was his son Charlemagne*.

PÉRONNE

Town in northern France on the Somme river and site of a monastery founded by Irish monks at the shrine of Fursa*. Fursa's brother Ultan* was abbot there and it was known as *Peronna Scottorum* (Péronne of the Irish) until its destruction by Norsemen in 880.

PIRMIN

Eighth-century Irish monk who is credited with the foundation of two monasteries, one in Murbach in Alsace, the other in Reichenau*, the Bodensee island.

REGENSBURG (RATISBON)

Bavarian city also known by the French name of Ratisbon, which lies on the Danube about sixty-three miles northeast of Munich. It was the site of the Irish Benedictine monastery of Saint James which was built by Marianus Scottus* (Muiredach Macc Robartaig) in 1076. It became the mother house of other *Schottenklöster** ('Irish monasteries') in Würzburg*, Nürnberg*, Constance, Vienna* and Eichstatt.

REICHENAU

An island in the Bodensee (Lake Constance) in Switzerland known to the Romans as *Augia Dives.* It was the site of a monastery founded by an Irish monk called Pirmin who died *c.* 753. It was much frequented by Irish exiles and pilgrims in the early Middle Ages and thereby assembled one of the richest collections of Irish material in Europe. The monastery was closed in 1757 and its library material was taken to Karlsruhe and placed in the *Badische Landesbibliothek* (Baden State Library).

REIMS

French city eighty miles north-east of Paris, the cathedral of which was the traditional place for the coronation of French kings. Pepin the Short* appointed an Irish cleric called Abel as archbishop there in 744. In the ninth century it became the headquarters of a group of Irish scholars and one of them, Dunchad, became the second Irishman to rule the archiepiscopal see.

ROSMORKYN

Site on the north-east coast of Scotland in modern Caithness of a Columban abbey founded by the seventh-century Irish monk, Curitan. Little is known about him except that he was at Birr in 697 when the *Cáin Adamnáin* was promulgated.

SCHOTTENKLÖSTER

Name of a number of continental Benedictine monasteries that, as the name implies, had a predominance of Irish monks. They originated in Ratisbon* where Marianus Scottus* built the Weih-Sankt-Peter monastery in 1076. These foundations continued to recruit largely from Ireland. During the twelfth century they showed the same signs of decay that seemed to afflict all religious houses. In an attempt to restore their earlier vigour, Innocent III (1198–1216) devised the congregation of *Schottenklöster* of which there were then nine member houses, which he placed under the authority of the abbot of Saint James of Ratisbon in 1215. A series of abbots tried without notable success to improve matters but their efforts were badly affected by a drop in recruitment and the devastation of the Black Death (1348–9). Numbers shrank to a handful in most monasteries. By 1500 few if any of the monks were Irish and deterioration continued. The 'Irish monasteries' were finally suppressed by Pius IX in 1862.

SEDULIUS SCOTTUS

From his name an Irishman, but nothing else is known about his early life. He arrived at Liège about 848 where he was welcomed by the bishop of the diocese, Hartgar. Like Eriugena* he was one of the circle of Charles the Bald* and was granted a 'grace-and-favour' house with a garden at Liège. Well educated and gifted with literary ability, he became a scholar courtier, famous for the excellence, ingenuity and variety of his Latin poems. In one eight-line *jeu d'esprit* he thanks a friend, Robert, for a gift of wine. In the verse, the second-declension name *Robertus* is used in each of its grammatical cases. Some scholars assign to him the famous

Gaelic poem about the cat Pangur Bán. His prose works include grammars, scriptural commentaries and a handbook for his royal master *On Christian Rulers*. His temperament was epicurean rather than ascetic, although he and his circle, which included an Irish priest, were almost certainly celibate. Nothing more is heard of him after 860.

SAINT DENIS

Site near Le Bourget north of Paris of the medieval abbey which became the cemetery of French kings. It held the cell of Dungal* who lived there from 784 to 827.

SALZBURG

Central Austrian city, about 150 miles west of Vienna, famous as the birthplace of Mozart. The Irishman Fergal, known in Austria as Virgil*, was appointed abbot of Saint Peter's monastery there by Duke Odilo of Bavaria in 742.

SANKT GALLEN

Swiss city about forty-five miles east of Zürich called after Columban's most important disciple Gall*, who refused to accompany his superior over the Alps to Italy. Gall stayed in the region near the Bodensee (Lake Constance) and gathered a community round him. After Gall's death (*c.* 630) a monastery bearing his name was established, taking the gentler Benedictine rule in 720 and lasting until its suppression in 1797. An Irishman, Moengal, became head of the school *c.* 850 and established the library, housing an outstanding collection of manuscripts written by Irish scribes.

These include illuminated gospel books and a ninth-century Priscian grammar, with some early Irish lyrics.

SAINT GOBAIN

Town in France fifteen miles west of Laon* now noted for glass production, near which the Irish monk Gobain kept his hermitage. He was a disciple of Fursa* and was murdered *c.* 670.

TARANTO

City in Apulia, the 'heel' of Italy, founded by the Spartans in the eighth century BC, taken from them by the Athenians and becoming the Roman Tarentum. In 1071, when the cathedral was being rebuilt, workmen discovered a sarcophagus containing the uncorrupted body of a man in episcopal vestments with the words *Cataldus Rachau* ('Cathald of Rathan') engraved on the pectoral cross. Miraculous cures followed and the relics were preserved in a shrine in a side chapel of the cathedral of Cathald* where they have been venerated since.

THEODORE OF CANTERBURY

Greek prelate born at Tarsus in Cicilia in Asia Minor *c.* 602. In 667 Pope Saint Vitalian appointed him personally to the English metropolitan see when he was over sixty and still not yet a priest. The effect of his work was remarkable. After a detailed tour of his province he filled all the vacant sees and in 672 called the first council of the whole English Church, still reeling from the dissension after the Synod of

Whitby*. It met at Hertford and concentrated upon the business of discipline and ecclesiastical organisation. His framework outlasted the Reformation of the sixteenth century and is still the basis of the diocesan system of the Church of England. He died in 690 at Canterbury.

TOURS

City of central France on the Loire and capital of the historical province of Touraine. It was the site of the monastery of Martin (315–97), the father of French monasticism and the first non-martyr to be venerated as a saint. His rule had a significant effect on the Irish Church, traditionally because of his influence upon Patrick but historically because Ninian* of *Candida Casa** 'learned' monasticism from him. Gregory of Tours (*c.* 538–94), the historian, author of the *History of the Franks,* was appointed bishop there in 573 and founded an important library. Alcuin*'s abbacy in 796 made it the great scholastic centre, after Aachen*, of the Carolingian empire. It was a place of resort of many Irish clerics and scholars during the ninth century and various manuscripts show Irish calligraphy and ornament.

ULTAN

Ultan was brother of Fursa* and Foillán* and went with them to Burgh Castle*, later joining Fursa in Lagny* and becoming abbot on his death. He succeeded as abbot of Péronne* after the murder of Foillan and remained there until his death in 686.

URSUS

Irish *peregrinus* who a century before the coming of Columban* established a monastery in Aosta on the Swiss/Italian border. He had worked in Digne in the south of France before crossing the Alps to preach against the Arian heresy that was strong in north Italy. He died in 595. His Latin name signifies 'bear' and the Irish equivalent would have been Mathgamain.

VIENNA

The *Schottenkloster* of Wien, which is dedicated to Our Lady, was founded by Duke Henry *c.* 1156. From it a daughter house was established at Kiev, the capital of modern Ukraine, but it was abandoned in 1241 because of the Mongol invasions. The present *Schottenkirche* is in the city centre of the Vienna on the Schottengasse and the abbey has the full title *Abtei Unserer Lieben-Frau zu den Schotten.*

VIRGIL

An Irish monk, Fergal, from Canice's monastery of Aghaboe, who was placed in charge of the diocese of Salzburg *c.* 740 by Pepin the Short. Since he was never ordained bishop and would not in humility ask to be, the sacramental duties were carried out by an Irish bishop called Dobdagrecus, the Latin version of Dub-dá-chrich. He was of an intellectually independent disposition, known as 'the Geometer', and was twice reported to Rome by Boniface of Mainz. His rather modern idea that 'there is below the earth another world', which implied the existence of other humans contemporary with Adam, shocked both Boniface and Pope Zachary. Virgil, whose general work of evangelising Carinthia was impeccable, remained doggedly as titular Bishop of Salzburg until he died in 784.

WHITBY

A town on the coast of Yorkshire about twenty miles northwest of Scarborough. The abbey (a 'double', housing both men and women religious) was founded by King Oswiu in thanksgiving for his defeat of the pagan Penda of Mercia. The first abbess was Hilda (614–80) and on her death Oswiu's daughter, Aelfflaed, ruled it in tandem with her mother, Eanflaed. The burial place of Caedmon (*fl.* 650–70), the first English poet to be known by name, it was the site of the famous synod of 664, which was called to settle differences between Celtic Church practice and that of Rome. The community of Lindisfarne*, as the premier English abbey of Celtic foundation, was to be greatly involved. The most obvious point at issue was the way of computing the date of Easter: Bede* records that at one point Oswiu, the Northumbrian king, had finished his Lenten fast and was celebrating Easter while his wife, Eanflaed, who was a Kentish princess and followed Augustine*'s Roman dating, was keeping Palm Sunday. This was just the kind of thing likely to confuse and scandalise new converts. The struggle went deeper than just dates and tonsures (another point of divergence); it was about central authority and local autonomy. Finan*, the abbot of Lindisfarne who succeeded Aidan, had stood out against the persuasions of Ronan, an Irish monk who had accepted the Roman system. On Finan's death in 661 he was replaced by Colman*, who took an even harder line. The opposing factions, the *Romani* and the *Hibernenses*, would have been recognisable by their haircuts. In the end, inevitably, the Roman party won, even though Hilda the hostess, as a client of Aidan, took the Celtic side. Oswiu, who presided, accepted the argument of Wilfrid who led for the Roman party that Colum Cille* had not the universal authority of Saint Peter. Colman would not accept the findings and led his monks with some English adherents to Ireland via Iona. Most of the southern Irish houses had conformed by 630 so the only diehards were to be found in Iona* Wales and parts of northern Ireland. All the Celtic foundations were in communion with Rome in these matters by the last quarter of the eighth century. It was the *peregrini* who unwittingly brought matters to a head. So long as the divergence was contained in Columban*'s island at 'the world's edge' where there was no strong central authority, either political or ecclesiastical, it could be tolerated. When the doughty Irish missionaries adamantly made the Celtic practices a part of the faith they preached outside Ireland and Scotland there was bound to be trouble. Whitby prevented a greater schism but the influence of a strong lay ruler was significant and a clash between the authority of Rome and that of equally pious and adamant local clerics remained a possibility until it became a reality in the sixteenth century.

WÜRZBURG

Bavarian city associated with Kilian*, who evangelised the Thuringians and the Franconians in the second half of the seventh century. His remains are enshrined in the crypt of the cathedral and it became a popular place of pilgrimage for Irish travellers. Clement Scottus* died there in the ninth century and it was there that Marianus Scottus*, the chronicler, was ordained priest in 1059 prior to his immediate immurement. A scholar, known only as David Scottus, was master of the cathedral school under Emperor Henry V (1081–1125) and accompanied his master on his Italian expedition to write a history of it. In the eleventh century there was a considerable Irish community there and in 1138–9 the *Scottenkloster* was built. It remained in Irish Benedictine hands until 1497.

SELECT BIBLIOGRAPHY

Anderson, A. O. and M. O. (eds. and trans.) Adomnán's *Vita Columbae.* London, 1961.

Attwater, D. *The Penguin Dictionary of Saints.* Harmondsworth, 1965 (Revised C. R. John, 1983.)

Boylan, H. *A Dictionary of Irish Biography.* Dublin, 1988.

Bradley, T. and Walsh, J. R. *A History of the Irish Church: 400–700 AD.* Dublin, 1991.

Brady, A. M. and Cleeve, B. *A Biographical Dictionary of Irish Writers.* Mullingar, 1985.

Concannon, H. *The Life of St Columban.* Dublin, 1915.

Flanagan, L. *A Chronicle of Irish Saints.* Belfast, 1990.

Kenney, J. F. *The Sources for the Early History of Ireland, Ecclestical: An Introduction and Guide.* New York, 1929. (Reissued Dublin, 1979.)

Marsden, J. *The Illustrated Colmcille.* London, 1991.

Martin, F. X. and Moody, T. H. (eds.) *The Course of Irish History.* Cork, 1967. (Revised edition, 1994.)

McNeill, J. T. *The Celtic Churches.* Chicago, 1974.

Montague, H. P. *The Saints and Martyrs of Ireland.* Gerrard's Cross, 1981.

Ó Fiaich, T. *Columbanus in His Own Words.* Dublin, 1974.

Ó Fiaich, T. *Irish Cultural Influence in Europe.* Cork, 1971.